The Garden Bi

Contents

The Revolution In Your Garden

Many of our most familiar birds are suffering because of changes in farming. Hundreds of thousands of miles of hedgerows, vital as nesting sites, have been ripped out and ponds have been drained.

Until recently, many seed-eating birds would forage for food in stubble fields throughout the dark, difficult days of winter. Now they don't get the chance, as the sowing of cereal crops in autumn becomes more and more common.

This assault on birdlife is taking a heavy toll, and it is not only singing Skylarks and colourful Yellowhammers which are suffering massive population crashes. Numbers of once-common species, such as Starlings and Song Thrushes, are also plummeting – and that is why gardens are assuming a more and more important role in terms of habitat.

Destruction of natural habitat means that, increasingly, wild birds struggle to survive.

Photo: Gareth Thomas FRPS

A Place Of Refuge

Desperate bird species are turning to gardens as a refuge from the unsympathetic countryside, and if you are prepared to feed them regularly, provide a supply of clean water and even plant trees and put up nestboxes, you will reap ample rewards.

In my own 20m x 20m back garden, just a mile from Peterborough city centre, we feed the birds all year (apart from August/September when wild food is readily available), and attract around 26 different species on a regular basis.

As the editor of Britain's most popular birdwatching magazine, I receive many letters from readers wanting to express the sheer pleasure they get from watching birds in their gardens. I hope this guide will encourage you to do a little bit more for wild birds – so that you too can benefit from their songs, their colour and their endlessly fascinating behaviour.

Attracting birds to your garden provides a great source of pleasure.

When To Feed

Traditionally, it is when snow lies thick and the ground is frozen, that the nation's bird-lovers start to put out food in the garden, but recently there has been a growing trend to provide provisions all year round.

Is it necessary or desirable to feed birds throughout the summer months? The British Trust for Ornithology has conducted studies which show that Greenfinches and Goldfinches suffer many casualties in spring, when exhausted adults cannot find enough natural food to sustain themselves or their broods.

By providing a reliable source of sunflower seeds or peanuts, you can clearly swing the balance back in favour of the birds. With their own food supplies secure, the adults can forage for caterpillars, grubs and insects to feed to their young.

Formerly wild birds only needed feeding in harsh winter conditions.

With their own food supply secure, adult birds are free to forage for their young.

Safeguards

Critics of summer feeding point out that chicks of Blue Tits and Great Tits have been found dead in their nest boxes, having choked on whole peanuts. Ornithologists believe that the adult birds would have only fed their chicks with nuts when natural soft foods, such as caterpillars, were unavailable, and they were at risk of dying of starvation anyway.

To safeguard young birds from such potential misfortunes, it is important to ensure that nuts are contained within wire mesh feeders.

The BTO recommends reducing the amount of food you supply in the autumn months (August to October). Naturally available seeds and berries are at their peak, and easing back will guard against the local birds becoming too dependent on you.

Choosing Equipment

Have you ever considered eating soup with your fingers or trying to get through steak with a spoon? No, of course not. We have learnt to use the appropriate utensils and dishes for our own food, and it makes sense to provide the same for your garden birds.

Nut Feeders

Peanuts should never ever be made available as whole nuts in case they choke young birds. There have been cases where desperate Blue Tits, unable to find enough juicy, green caterpillars in cold wet springs, have taken whole peanuts to their starving broods with disastrous results.

The ideal peanut dispenser should be a tube made from rust-proof metal mesh, or if you live in a squirrel-free zone, from red plastic mesh bags. Both will ensure that the birds can only peck small pieces.

Photo: Gareth Thomas FRPS

Plastic-covered metal peanut feeder.

If you feel the tits in your garden suffer unfairly from more aggressive species on the main feeder, look out for small wooden feeders with a sliding mesh panel on the bottom. Only the agile tits can hang upside-down to get at food from these dispensers.

A squirrel-proof nut feeder.

This nut feeder can be attached to a window.

Cage Feeders

If squirrels are a pest, then invest in a protected cage feeder. Though more expensive, the best of their kind will prove wise investments. Even the most persistent offenders will eventually give up trying to chew their way through the steel bars.

Seed Feeders

The best seed dispensers are clear, polycarbonate tubes with varying numbers of portholes at intervals down the side. Ensure there is a protective lip at each hole to prevent seed spilling out, and rain spoiling the food inside. A short perch makes it easy for the finches to reach the seed easily.

Plastic seed feeder with four portholes.

If you are going away for a period of time, a large capacity seed feeder will ensure the food supply is maintained.

Most seed feeders have a metal loop or handle so that they can be hung from the bird table or the branches of a tree. Alternatively, you can buy ones that can be fixed to a window with sucker cups.

Choose the location with care and you will be able to enjoy super close-up views, particularly of Robins, and Blue and Great Tits.

Another clear, plastic feeder that can be stuck to the kitchen window is shaped like a small house. Birds can enter freely through large circular holes, and because the whole thing is transparent, you will be able to see all activity very clearly. Generally speaking, the birds will not be disturbed by your presence inside the house, once they have got used to the location.

Bird Tables

If you are likely to have lots of kitchen scraps to give away, then a covered bird table can be a valuable asset, and even the most ham-fisted handyperson should have no trouble building one. Ensure your wood (preferably 9 mm thick plywood) is waterproofed, but do not use creosote as this is poisonous to birds.

To ensure seed and crumbs do not get blown away, fix battens to the base-board, but make sure there is a 3 mm gap at each corner so that rain water can drain away freely.

The roof should be angled, and overhang the base-board to prevent rain spoiling the food. Many pet shops and garden centres have ready-made bird tables for sale if you are not into carpentry. Expect to pay a minimum of £20 for a decent flat-pack model, but a robust, squirrel-proof construction could set you back at least £100.

A hanging bird table.

Choosing Equipment

Roofed bird table, supported on a post.

You can hang a bird table on wires from the branch of a tree or mount it on a post, but make sure the latter is sturdy enough to withstand high winds. To prevent cats and squirrels leaping up to the food tray, it is a good idea to make a wide collar (something like an old dustbin lid) to go underneath.

Fat Dispensers

A number of do-it-yourself options are open to you – or you can take the easy route and buy ready-prepared food bars, which combine animal fats, nuts, seeds, and sometimes, even insects.

If you fancy doing your own thing, half a coconut shell (or a ceramic tit bell) can be filled with a mixture of suet, lard, dried fruit and seeds. Fix a wire through the shell and hang upside-down to prevent the rain spoiling the contents.

Alternatively, you can hang up a log feeder from a wire hook. Select a piece of wood and drill a series of holes about 6 mm deep and 3 mm wide. Pack each hole with suet, fat or birdcake mix.

When I was in Arizona recently, I came across a local birdwatcher who nailed halves of oranges to tree branches in his garden. When all the fruit segments had been eaten, he replaced them with peanut butter – and the birds loved it!

Water Containers

It is probably more important for you to provide a reliable source of clean water than food for the welfare of your garden birds. The dry nature of seeds means that finches, sparrows and doves need to drink at regular intervals, and many species need to bathe regularly to keep their feathers in tip-top condition.

An ornamental bird bath can be a beautiful addition to a garden, but if finances are tight, simply use a large, but shallow, plastic plant-pot drip saucer. Don't forget to weigh it down with a heavy stone.

A terracotta bell which can be filled with a food mix.

A regular supply of fresh water is essential.

Good Housekeeping

DID YOU KNOW?

Spotted Flycatchers are among the last migrants to arrive from Africa each year. This is because they rely on large flying insects, such as bees and flies, which are not generally available before the end of May.

Here are a few key tips to make sure your garden birds stay healthy:

• Scrub down bird tables at least once a week with disinfectant, and rinse clean.

• Scrape unused food and bird droppings into a plastic bag and put them in the dustbin. Droppings can infect food items and lead to salmonella poisoning.

• Never serve mouldy or salty foods.

• Serve food in small amounts; excess food is likely to attract rats and mice at night.

• Move bird tables and feeder poles at regular intervals to prevent a build-up of droppings on the ground.

• Be careful where you site feeders. Do not place them close to trees or bushes which may conceal a cat.

Be careful not to site feeders near bushes or trees which could provide a good hiding place for a cat.

Like all wild creatures, birds essentially have very few needs: a reliable source of fresh food and water; a safe environment to raise their young; and suitable places to hide from predators. Even the smallest garden can be developed to provide food and shelter, though tiny town gardens may not be suitable for nestboxes.

The power of flight makes birds very mobile and they will adopt your garden (if you have made it attractive enough) as part of a much bigger feeding area.

Flocks of Blue Tits and Great Tits will complete a circuit of neighbouring gardens several times a day to exploit

DID YOU KNOW?

You can help discover more about garden birds by joining the British Trust for Ornithology's Garden BirdWatch scheme. For full details call 01842 750 050.

Even a total newcomer to birdwatching will have no difficulty identifying the large pinkish-brown Jay, with eye-catching bright blue wing patches and bold white rump. Be aware that the Jay may predate the eggs and chicks of smaller birds in spring and summer.

Photo: Gareth Thomas FRPS

the richest available feeding. By varying the times they spend in one place, they are also able to cut down the risk of being attacked by a cat, a Sparrowhawk or other predator.

Nestboxes are better suited to a larger garden.

Counting Heads

It is surprising just how many individual birds are likely to visit your feeders each day. Experts estimate that if you count the number of Blue Tits you can see at one time – and then multiply that figure by ten – that will be an accurate estimate of how many birds of that species you are helping to sustain each day.

Let us look at the different types of food you can provide for wild birds and the species that you are likely to attract. Bear in mind that birds are adaptable creatures, and they are quite likely to exploit more than one source of food. You will be amazed at how quickly some insect-eaters, such as Long-tailed Tits, have learnt to come to birdfeeders.

You will be amazed at the number of birds that come to feed.

Peanut Power

Peanuts, which are not a nut but a type of legume (pea/bean family), have dominated the bird feeding scene for many years. They are rich in oil and protein, which birds need to produce energy and body heat, and a wide range of birds love them.

A few years ago, a lot of low-quality peanuts were being sold as birdfood, and sadly many supplies were tainted with aflatoxin, a natural fungus which so damages a bird's immune system that many deaths occurred.

Happily, the Birdfood Standards Association was formed to police supplies around the world and any peanuts bearing their logo 'We're Safe Nuts' will be aflatoxin-free.

Although it is more cost-effective to buy peanuts in bulk, make sure you can store them in a cool, dry place and protect them from mice or other rodents.

Let's have a closer look at some of the bird species that will flock in for peanuts.

Large peanuts, rich in oil, and free from aflatoxin contamination.

Standard peanuts – slightly smaller in size.

Peanut granules – higher in protein and oil content. Feed little and often.

Great Spotted Woodpecker

(Dendrocropos major)

If your garden is anywhere near woodland, you may be able to attract this handsome bird to the nut feeder– and to animal fat smeared on tree branches. This is more likely to happen in winter when normal food (insects, seeds and nuts) is in short supply, but in my own garden we get both male and female birds at different times of the year.

During summer, the male bird (identified by the red patch on the back of the head) will attack the peanuts for minutes on end, and fly off with as much as it can carry to its tree hole to feed the female sitting on eggs, and later the young birds themselves. I have even seen a young woodpecker sitting on the arm of our feeder, waiting for its father to extract peanut fragments and feed them to it.

Great Spotted Woodpeckers are extremely wary and will not tolerate other birds on the feeder. They do not occur in Ireland and are extremely rare in Scotland.

Blue Tit *(Parus caerleus)*
and Great Tit *(Parus major)*

Acrobatic Blue Tits and Great Tits were among the first species to appreciate the food value of peanuts, though they will also take a great many other foods too. Their small bills can cope with either the wire-mesh feeders or the red, plastic bag type.

Peanut Power

Blue Tit.

If you find that larger species are bullying the tits, here is a possible solution. Buy unshelled peanuts and thread them on to a piece of garden twine. The feather-light Blue Tits and Great Tits will be able to extract the kernels which other larger, more clumsy birds will have to ignore.

A word of warning: do not go to this trouble if you have squirrels in the neighbourhood, as they will demolish the lot in a very short time.

Long-Tailed Tit *(Aegithalos caudatus)*

In more recent times, engaging Long-tailed Tits have started to leave woodlands, and a purely insect diet, to feed on peanuts in gardens. In winter you may see several birds together – these will be parents and offspring from the previous season. They weigh so little that they need to huddle together on cold nights to stay alive.

In spring, you are more likely to see just a pair of adults come to the feeders. They are not shy birds and may let you get quite close. Look out for basically black, pink and cream birds with an exceptionally long tail.

Jay *(Garrulus glandarius)*

Related to the crow, the handsome Jay shares their suspicious attitude towards man, so don't expect to see them on your main feeders. Try tempting them into your garden in winter with some strategically placed peanuts, as they look to augment their normal diet of acorns. Look around the more secluded corners of your garden for crevices where you can wedge nuts – tree bark is often suitable.

Siskin *(Carduelis spinus)*

The Siskin is a delicate green, yellow and black finch that breeds in coniferous forests. However, in late winter, when its natural food of alder cones are in short supply, it will readily come to gardens, where it shows a marked preference for the red, plastic nut-bags. (Does it think they are giant alder cones?)

Nuthatch *(Sitta europea)*

Though primarily another woodland insect-eater, the Nuthatch will often visit rural gardens in winter looking for seeds and peanuts. Not only will it eat at the feeders, but if supplies are plentiful, it will fly off with food to hoard.

A beautiful orange body is set off by blue-grey upperparts, white throat and a strong black eye stripe, but its looks are not the Nuthatch's most distinctive feature. It is equipped with incredibly strong claws that enable it to walk up and down tree-trunks in search of insects hiding in the bark.

Super Sunflowers

Sunflower seeds, both black and striped, are now probably the most popular bird food you can offer your feathered guests. Like peanuts they are rich in oil, protein and vitamins, and the birds find the husks are relatively easy to take off.

Let's have a look at some other species you can expect to attract.

Black sunflower seeds – the most cost effective means of supplying high-energy food.

Coal Tit *(Parus ater)*

If you live near conifer trees, you have a good chance of attracting Coal Tits, particularly in winter when their preferred insect food is not so readily available. But be warned, there is a price to pay for enjoying their acrobatic antics. The Coal Tit is a great food hoarder (part of its technique for surviving harsh winters), and it will dig little holes

Sunflower hearts – the highest energy food available.

all over your garden to bury seeds. It can come as a bit of a surprise to suddenly notice a 30 cm sunflower powering from the midst of a hanging basket!

You can identify the Coal Tit easily from its warm-brown body colour and a distinctive white patch on the back of the head and neck.

Greenfinch *(Carduelis chloris)*

A chunky green and yellow bird, with a distinctive wheezy song, and a sizeable seed-eater's bill, the Greenfinch is likely to be the most common visitor to your sunflower dispenser. These birds are great fun to watch as they are constantly battling with each other, and with smaller species, for the best feeding positions. Through binoculars you can study how they rotate the seeds in their beaks to remove the thin husk.

If you have dense conifers in the garden or close by, you are quite likely to have Greenfinches nesting in them. Eggs are laid in April, and feeding the chicks places a great strain on the parents as they struggle to find any wild seed for themselves so early in the year. Garden feeders can make all the difference, so don't rush to remove your sunflower supply.

The male Greenfinch has a smooth yellowish-green plumage with bright-yellow wing panels and a black tail. The female is more mottled and subdued in colouring, though still with an overall greenish appearance.

Goldfinch *(Carduelis carduelis)*

One bird that many people are surprised to see on their seed and nut feeders is the Goldfinch. Its delicate fine-pointed bill has developed specially to exploit seeds (such as teasel and forget-me-not) which are too small and difficult for other birds to eat.

However, during recent years, it has increasingly flocked into gardens and has learnt to battle for peanuts and seeds with its larger cousins. It is a feisty little bird and will often send a bigger bird fleeing.

Its eye-catching red and black face and bright-yellow wing patches makes the Goldfinch instantly recognisable. You can also listen for the typical musical tinkling song – they may be in your area even if you have not seen them on the feeders yet. Encourage them to your garden by planting up a wild area with thistles, teasels and other wild flowers, and let them form seed.

Seeds And Grains

High-energy seed suitable for year-round feeding.

Summer seed, useful during breeding and moulting.

A mix of sunflowers, peanut granules, pinhead oatmeal, millet, canary seed, maize, and wheat, suitable throughout the year.

Designed to use in tube feeders, this mix is free-flowing, high in oil, and contains no cereal.

Many of the commonest species to visit gardens thrive on oil-rich seeds and cereal grains, and there are many mixtures you can buy for both summer and winter feeding. Common ingredients will include oatmeal, millet, maize, sunflowers, hemp, linseed and canary seed. Niger seeds (from the Indian ramtil plant) and thistle seeds which particularly appeal to Goldfinches, are generally only available from specialist suppliers.

All these seeds are rich sources of fats, carbohydrates, minerals and vitamins, but you will have to experiment with different brands of mixed seed to discover which best suit your garden birds. Some cheaper mixes contain a high proportion of hard-shelled seeds which will be ignored, so don't invest in a large amount until you have tested it.

By providing a mix of seeds at ground level you will attract birds such as Chaffinches (and their rarer cousins, Bramblings), Robins, Dunnocks, Blackbirds and Starlings, while Collared Doves and Wood Pigeons will gobble up vast amounts of grain.

Chaffinches, Greenfinches, House Sparrows and Wood Pigeons will tend to consume any seed that comes their way, while Siskins seem to share the Goldfinches' enthusiasm for the tiny oil-rich niger seeds.

Collared Dove

(Streptopelia decaocto)
The mournful cooing of
Collared Doves sounds in
towns and villages
throughout the British
Isles, and yet only 50 years
ago the species was
unknown here. But when
you realise that it will lay a
second clutch of two eggs
while still feeding the first
chicks – and that five broods a year are not uncommon – it is
easy to appreciate how this particular population boom has
come about.

Look closely to appreciate the dusky pink-grey plumage
(males and females look the same), and note the black neck
ring edged with white that gives the species its name. Though
too big to balance on the perches of a tubular feeder, the
Collared Dove will hoover up vast quantities of seed from the
ground or bird table.

Wood Pigeon *(Columba palumbus)*

A pair of stocky Wood Pigeons in the garden should ensure
that very little seed which spills from a bird table goes to
waste. They have a ferocious appetite and will eat a wide
variety of foods, including berries and plant shoots, as well as
cereals and seeds.

Close-up views reveal a subtle but beautiful plumage that
ranges from pink on the breast to mauve and grey. There are
large white patches on the side of the neck, and, when it flies,
the Wood Pigeon displays a distinctive white wing bar.

Seeds And Grains

Robin *(Erithacus rubecula)*

Britain's national bird presents no identification problems, though you may be foxed when you see your first juvenile bird. Instead of the familiar red breast, baby Robins are camouflaged in brown spotty garb. Continental Robins come to Britain to escape harsh weather, so don't presume your wintering pair is the same one that bred during the summer.

Robins live on insects for most of the year, and will greatly appreciate live food, such as meal worms, if you can obtain a supply. It is best not to feed fishermen's maggots.

Dunnock *(Prunella modularis)*

Once known as the Hedge Sparrow, and now called a Hedge Accentor in some quarters, the Dunnock is our most overlooked garden bird. One glance at the thin, pointed bill is enough to tell it apart from the House Sparrow or the female finches.

Like a little grey-headed brown mouse, it probes in and around garden plants and leaf litter looking for insects and grubs, but will happily pick up seeds and fragments of peanuts that fall from the birdfeeders.

Chaffinch *(Fringilla coelebs)*

Most of Britain's birds tend to be rather plain, but a cock Chaffinch in breeding plumage is a real treat for the eye. The pinkish-orange face, chest and belly are noticed first, but there is also a blue-grey head and brown back. The features to look for when the birds fly are bold, white wing bars and a greenish rump.

Some people confuse female Chaffinches with female House Sparrows. It is true that both are brownish, but the sparrow lacks any white in the wing.

Traditionally foragers on winter farmland, Chaffinches in our garden have learnt to hang on to nut feeders as well as picking up mixed seed from bird tables and the ground.

Female Chaffinch.

Brambling *(Fringilla montifringilla)*

It is easy to see that this bird is a close relative of the Chaffinch, but most birdwatchers would be overjoyed to get one in their garden. Bramblings breed in Scandinavia and Siberia, and they spend the winter in places where they are likely to find plenty of their favourite food – beech mast. This means that in some years Britain attracts very few birds, while in others, when the beech trees have been very productive, there can be massive influxes into our woodlands between October and April.

In severe winters, natural food supplies may be exhausted and that is when you are most likely to see Bramblings in your garden, looking for seed on the ground.

The male bird looks similar to his Chaffinch cousin, but the breast and shoulder colour is orange. The head is black, streaked with grey in early winter, and it displays a prominent white rump in flight. The same goes for the female and helps separate her from a female Chaffinch. Overall, the female Brambling does not look as dull as her cousin.

Fulsome Fat Feeders

You can make your own fat-bar, or you can buy them ready-made.

If you are a dab hand in the kitchen, why not have a go at making your own fat-bar? Simply melt beef-suet in a saucepan, and then add seeds, grain and dried fruit to soak up the fat. Press it into empty yoghurt containers, insert loops of garden wire, and then place in your fridge to harden.

After about three hours the mixture will be hard enough to extract, and you can then hang the fat-bars by the wire loop from tree branches or your feeder arms. If all this seems a lot of trouble, you will be pleased to learn that your local pet food suppliers or supermarket can offer a range of commercially-produced products.

These high-value foods will be especially appreciated by the smaller species, such as tits, Robins and finches. Bigger birds, such as Starlings and Blackbirds, are unlikely to be able to hang on to such slippery fare.

However, if you would like to attract woodpeckers and perhaps Nuthatch, try smearing a fat mixture into the bark of tree branches.

This is a peanut cake, made from beef-suet and peanut flour.

Blackcap (male).

Blackcap *(Sylvia atricapella)*

Warblers traditionally migrate south to the Mediterranean or Africa for the winter, but increasing numbers of attractive Blackcaps now spend this time with us. Milder winters mean they can find some insect food, and they supplement this with provided fruit and fat-bars.

These birds are not our own summering ones, but incoming migrants from Germany and central Europe. The male bird sports the black cap that gives the species its name, and while the female shares the grey body and brownish upperparts, its cap is brown.

DID YOU KNOW?

The nest of the Long-tailed Tit is a marvellously domed structure made of moss and cobwebs that can stretch as the chicks grow inside. It is lined with hundreds of feathers and camouflaged with lichen on the outside.

Full-Value Fruit

If you are lucky enough to have an apple tree, you will be aware of how popular the fruit is with Blackbirds, Song and Mistle Thrushes and, maybe, those attractive winter visitors from Scandinavia, Redwings and Fieldfares.

Store apples and pears in a cool, dry place, and put them out on the ground when winter weather starts to bite. Grapes are another popular fruit with many birds – if you can afford such luxuries.

Blackbird *(Turdus merula)*

This woodland species is one of the most successful garden birds, finding worms in lawns, insects in shrubs, and berries (guard those raspberries!). Adult males are all black with a bright yellow bill, but females, which may incubate up to five broods a year, are a less eye-catching brown.

Although they will eat a wide variety of birdfoods, Blackbirds are appreciative of apples, pears and grapes in winter.

A Blackbird feeding from windfall apples.

Song Thrush

(Turdus philomelos)
Encourage a Song Thrush into
your garden with apples and
other fruits, and it's likely to
repay you by eating the snails
that devastate lettuce and other
crops. Sadly, seeing a Song Thrush gets increasingly difficult
as the population is in steep decline.

Plain brown on the back, it has small neat spots on its breast
and belly. Listen for its rich song, which features repeated
phrases.

Redwing *(Turdus iliacus)*

Plant pyracantha and cotoneaster bushes in your garden and
you may, one day, be rewarded with a sighting of this
attractive thrush feeding on the berries in winter. It spends the
summer breeding in Scandinavia but comes across the North
Sea in large flocks to escape the cold. Providing apples and
other soft fruits can be a lifesaver for them.

The smallest British thrush, the Redwing has a bold, cream
stripe above the eye and a rust-red flash down the flanks,
which shows up well in flight.

Fieldfare *(Turdus pilaris)*

Another visitor from Scandinavia, the Fieldfare is a bigger,
chunkier bird than the Redwing. Its most prominent features
are a grey head and rump, rich brown back and a spotted
yellow front, which positively glows in bright sunlight.

Though it mixes freely with Redwings, it is only likely to
follow them into gardens during very severe weather. Again,
it shares a liking for apples and garden berries.

Superior Scraps

Birds will happily feed off the scraps from the kitchen, but be careful not to offer them items that are mouldy, too dry, too spicy or too salty. Stale bread, a staple of omnivorous species such as House Sparrows and Starlings, should be soaked to ensure it is not too hard.

Starling.

Fatty cooked bacon-rind is a good food as long as it is not too salty, and cheese is another high-fat food that will be much appreciated. If you crumble the cheese into small pieces and scatter it among your garden plants, it can be picked up by Wrens and Robins without competition from more aggressive species.

Other suitable food for bird tables includes:
Cooked potatoes: Starlings love spuds.
Cooked rice: Boil without salt.
Dog food: This nutritious source of food is popular with a variety of species.
Dried fruit: Robins and thrushes enjoy sultanas and raisins, but will appreciate the fruit being soaked in water to soften it.
Suet: A life-saver in long, cold winters.

Starling *(Sturnus vulgaris)*

Some people dislike the raucous, squabbling Starling but it is one of my favourite species. Seen at close quarters, or through binoculars, the feathers show a whole range of iridescent colours. In the winter, this is enhanced by bold, white breast spots. If you want to tell the sexes apart in spring, look at the colour at the base of the bill – it's blue for boys and pink for girls.

If you hear odd bird sounds around your garden, the chances are it's a Starling. They are incredible mimics and not only impersonate other bird species, but even the sound of a telephone ringing.

Jackdaw *(Corvus monedula)*

The smallest member of the British crow family has adjusted well to urban situations, and many pairs hijack domestic chimney-pots as a nesting hole. Apart from its size, the Jackdaw's most striking feature is the pale eye and the grey patch on the back of the head.

An adaptable bird, it feeds on grains, fruits and insects and will be tempted by a wide variety of kitchen scraps.

House Sparrow *(Passer domesticus)*

It surprises many people to learn that House Sparrows are not our most common bird, and that their numbers are declining rapidly in rural areas. They are familiar to us because of their ability to occupy the human environment, nesting in houses or gardens. They feed on a broad range of foods provided by man, as well as their traditional diet of insects in summer and grain in winter.

The male sports a grey crown and greyish underparts, while the black bib contrasts with paler cheek patches. The back is a mix of rich browns and black. The female has similar back patterning, though the colours are duller and she lacks bib or pale cheek patches.